SELF-DISCOVERY JOURNAL
FOR FIRST-TIME MOMS

SELF-DISCOVERY JOURNAL

FOR
FIRST-TIME
MOMS

REFLECT, RECORD, AND
RECONNECT WITH YOU

SARAH GRIESEMER, PHD

ROCKRIDGE
PRESS

Interior and Cover Designer: Stephanie Sumulong
Art Producer: Sarah Feinstein
Editor: Adrian Potts
Production Editor: Emily Sheehan
Production Manager: Holly Haydash

Photography used under license from iStock.com. Author photo courtesy of St. Laurent Photography.

ISBN: Print 978-1-64876-956-6 | eBook 978-1-64876-957-3

R0

"FIND OUT
WHO YOU ARE
AND DO IT
ON PURPOSE."

DOLLY PARTON

CONTENTS

INTRODUCTION

If no one has said it to you yet, let me be the first to offer congratulations on the birth of your motherhood! As a licensed
psychologist working with mothers in my private practice, I
spend a great deal of time helping new moms uncover their
new selves. We explore the new mother part of them and
discuss how it fits in with their other identities; what has
changed and stayed the same in terms of their roles, dreams,
values, and priorities. With love and attention, this process of
uncovering can feel spacious and comfortable. I am so excited
to help you on this journey of self-discovery.

My professional life focuses on new mothers, largely
because of my own complicated transition to becoming a
mother. In hindsight, I realize that I spent a lot of time pre-
paring for the arrival of my first child but gave very little
attention to becoming a mother. After I gave birth, I had no
women elders around me helping me to make sense out of
the feelings I was having. I felt intense love for my child and
equally intense loneliness. I experienced joy and confidence
in some of my mothering skills, as well as frustration and
powerlessness that left me in tears. I wanted to do everything
myself, and yet I resented not having more help. I wanted to
return to work, and also felt guilty for leaving my child. I des-
perately needed someone to help me unpack all the conflicting
thoughts and feelings that were emerging.

My hope is that I can be that someone for you: Together we
will explore who you are now, as a mother, in all its complexity.
I am a therapist because I believe storytelling is incredibly
healing. In this journal, you will have a chance to tell your
story. You can use this space to feel inspired, find comfort,
purge pain, explore the meaning behind your thoughts and
feelings, and learn self-care practices.

Of course, while this space is a beautiful opportunity to
process sadness, guilt, anxiety, and fear, it may not be enough

support for some. Please see the Resources section (page 166) to find out when and how to get support for feelings that are making it difficult for you to rest, sleep, leave the house, or perform normal daily functions.

How to Use This Journal

I feel such joy and warmth thinking about you using this journal. My hope is that you can feel my care for you in these pages. Each themed section includes a variety of prompts, exercises, positive affirmations, and powerful quotes to help guide you through the process of discovering who you are as a new mom. Take your time; there is no rush to the finish, because we are always changing and evolving. I recommend that you start with the first section, "Meet Yourself Where You Are" (page 1), and end with the final section, "The Path Forward" (page 139), and complete the pages in those sections in order. Beyond that, there is no correct order for completing the journal. Feel free to listen to your gut and move to the sections that call out to you.

Before we begin, take a moment to consider how to create space for this meaningful process. Intentionally set aside time to devote to the process. Ask someone to watch your child every evening for a few minutes so you can have alone time to reflect; or if you need extended time to focus and get in the flow, perhaps block off a chunk of time once a week to be child-free. Or if you are a fly-by-the-seat-of-your-pants gal, you might fit in your time whenever you have a moment. I urge you right now to decide what will work best for you and take steps to make it happen.

I am excited for you to begin this amazing and life-changing journey of discovering your new self. May you enter with a soft and open heart in appreciation of giving yourself the gift of love.

"THE TRUE
SUCCESS IS NOT
ALWAYS FOUND IN
ACCOMPLISHING
YOUR GOAL.
SOMETIMES
IT'S IN THE WAY
THE PROCESS
CHANGES YOU."

EMILY MAROUTIAN

MEET YOURSELF WHERE YOU ARE

We often think of ourselves as static beings that stay the same over time. The truth is that we are constantly changing: our priorities, our emotions, our bodies, our thoughts. Taking time to get to know yourself in this moment of becoming a mother allows you the space to make meaningful decisions based on what you need now, not what you needed when you were childless.

I invite you to make yourself a cup of tea, pull up a chair, and get to know yourself with the curiosity and warmth you would offer a new friend. It is by offering our true selves self-compassion and understanding that we create more room to love and care for others.

Take a moment to gather up items that bring you nurturance and joy, such as a cozy blanket, pictures of loved ones, a piece of art you love, a pretty plant, or a pillow to cuddle against. Leave these items in your journaling space so you can return here and always find uplifting and comforting surroundings to settle into. If you won't be journaling in one spot, you might gather them into a bag or a basket for easy transport.

Setting intentions helps us get clear on what we are hoping to receive. What feelings, experiences, learning, or thoughts do you want to make yourself open to receiving in this process of journaling? Your intentions could be broad, such as "I would like to feel calm," or specific, such as "I want to discover what I am good at as a mother."

_____

_____

_____

_____

_____

_____

_____

_____

_____

_____

_____

_____

_____

_____

_____

_____

_____

_____

Identify Your Values

Part of our exploration in this journal, and in life, is in how to live out our days while staying in alignment with our values. Take a moment to reflect on the values you want to keep central to your daily living. Circle three to five values below that are most important to you.

→ Achievement
→ Adventure
→ Authenticity
→ Authority
→ Autonomy
→ Balance
→ Boldness
→ Community
→ Compassion
→ Competency
→ Courage
→ Creativity
→ Curiosity
→ Determination
→ Fairness
→ Faith
→ Family
→ Fun
→ Growth
→ Happiness
→ Honesty
→ Humor
→ Influence
→ Inner harmony
→ Justice

→ Kindness
→ Leadership
→ Learning
→ Love
→ Loyalty
→ Meaningful work
→ Openness
→ Optimism
→ Peace
→ Play
→ Pleasure
→ Recognition
→ Relationships
→ Reputation
→ Respect
→ Responsibility
→ Security
→ Self-respect
→ Service
→ Spirituality
→ Stability
→ Success
→ Trustworthiness
→ Wealth
→ Wisdom

One of the main tasks of motherhood is learning to surrender. You may be faced with surrendering control over how your body looks, how your child behaves, what other people think of you, or how your day will be scheduled. Write down what comes to mind for the following prompts:

What role has control played in your life?

_____

_____

_____

_____

How have you experienced surrendering control as a new mother?

_____

_____

_____

_____

_____

_____

_____

_____

_____

_____

_____

Many new mothers feel as though they are in competition with other mothers or imagine that they are being judged. These critical thoughts often interfere with our ability to soften our hearts and feel self-compassion. Consider what critical thoughts you may be having and how you can soften them. What judgments have you had of yourself? What would a compassionate friend have said to you if they heard these things?

Releasing Judgment

Choose one judgment from the previous page that comes to mind frequently. Write it down on a sheet of paper. To release your judgment, tear up your paper and toss it to the wind for the birds to use for nests, burn it in your fireplace, bury it in your yard, or just throw it away. Whatever you choose, repeat this mantra several times aloud: "I release myself of this judgment. I am trying the best I can. I am held in compassion." Repeat this exercise whenever a judgmental thought becomes stuck in your head.

Often we have an idea of what motherhood will feel like, and that is rarely in line with the actual experience. What did you imagine you would be like as a new mother? Write about how your experience is different from—and also similar to—what you imagined.

If you are finding yourself feeling critical of or disappointed in the differences between what you expected motherhood to be like and how things actually are, take a moment to write to the disappointed part of yourself as though you were reassuring a sad friend. What would you say? What would you want them to know?

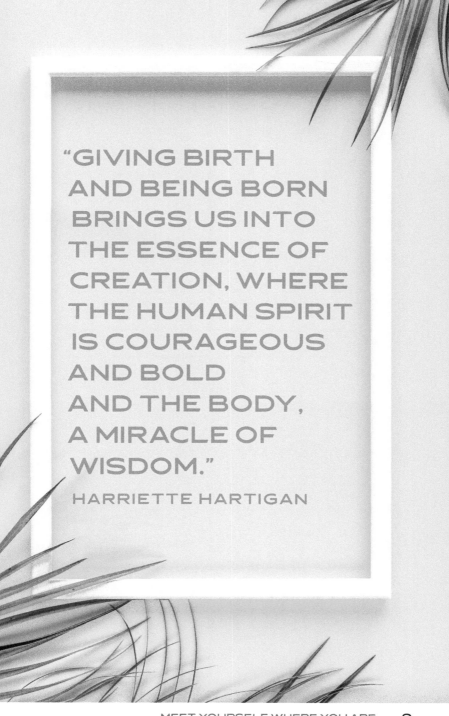

"GIVING BIRTH AND BEING BORN BRINGS US INTO THE ESSENCE OF CREATION, WHERE THE HUMAN SPIRIT IS COURAGEOUS AND BOLD AND THE BODY, A MIRACLE OF WISDOM."

HARRIETTE HARTIGAN

Introverts often feel replenished from being alone at home. Extroverts often feel restored by spending time in groups. Based on this idea, do you consider yourself an introvert or extrovert?

_____

_____

_____

_____

How well is the introverted/extroverted part of you being nourished right now?

_____

_____

_____

_____

_____

What do you need in order to feel more replenished?

_____

_____

_____

_____

_____

Our priorities often shift as we age. For example, when you have young children, you may choose to focus on family instead of career until the children are older. Spend a few moments taking stock of where you are and what you care about most right now, keeping in mind that your priorities can change again in the future. Firstly, write one goal you have for one year from now.

_____

_____

_____

_____

_____

_____

_____

Now, write down three goals for the next 5 to 10 years.

_____

_____

_____

_____

_____

_____

_____

_____

Seeing Is Believing

Gather two or three objects that represent what you want to focus on in your life right now. This might be a value such as "self-compassion" or a priority such as "self-care." Place them around your home in visible places as a reminder of your priorities. For example, above my sink I've placed plants to remind me to prioritize time in nature, and by my bedside I have a few trinkets gifted from friends to remind me of the importance of friendship in my life.

Who are "you" really? When you strip away your body, your possessions, your family, and your job, what are you left with? Some may consider themselves to be a soul, or sparks of energy, or their brain, or stardust. Sketch or describe your idea of what your "self" or "essence" is.

_____

_____

_____

_____

_____

_____

_____

_____

Because of the energy and work mothering young children requires, you will need more support at this stage of your life than ever before—especially in the form of self-care. What have you done to show love and care for yourself in the past day? What have you done to show love and care for others in the same timeframe? How balanced is your list?

Ways I have shown love and care for myself	Ways I have shown love and care for others

Brainstorm small ways you can show yourself love that you can do throughout the week. This could be anything you like, such as:

→ Turning on a song you love and dancing.

→ Lighting a candle and finding a comfortable place to sit. Set a timer for two minutes. While you watch the candle flicker, repeat to yourself, "I am made of stardust and light. I deserve deep and lasting love."

→ Ordering your favorite takeout for dinner, even if you have groceries in the fridge.

→ Taking a nap even though there are dishes in the sink and toys on the floor.

→ Buying pants that fit your current body and feel comfortable.

Write down a list of 10 actions you would like to take. Choose one from the list to do right now.

_____

_____

_____

_____

_____

_____

_____

_____

_____

_____

_____

_____

_____

Cultivating gratitude, even in the face of hardship and pain, helps create a state of lasting joy in our lives. List three things you feel grateful for right now.

_____
_____
_____
_____
_____
_____

Now list three (big or small) successes you have had this week that you are happy about or that make you feel proud of yourself.

_____
_____
_____
_____
_____
_____
_____
_____
_____
_____

Many mothers feel ashamed for not enjoying motherhood more, yet it is incredibly common after having a new child to be overwhelmed, frustrated, and disappointed. Whatever you are experiencing, remember that your feelings are valid and that they will pass.

How do you feel about your life right now? Are there more positives than negatives? Or is it the other way around?

_____

_____

_____

_____

_____

_____

_____

What are things that you have found disappointing that you thought you would like? After each disappointment, write "It is okay to feel disappointed even though I love my baby. This feeling will pass."

_____

_____

_____

_____

_____

_____

_____

Our vision of who we are can be changed by having a baby. What is one thing that has changed since having a child that surprises you? How do you feel about this change? What would it be like to accept this new part of your life?

_____

_____

_____

_____

_____

_____

_____

_____

_____

_____

_____

_____

_____

_____

_____

_____

_____

_____

"I STILL HAVE TO LEARN A BALANCE OF BEING THERE FOR [MY CHILD], AND BEING THERE FOR ME. I'M WORKING ON IT. I NEVER UNDERSTOOD WOMEN BEFORE, WHEN THEY PUT THEMSELVES IN SECOND OR THIRD PLACE. AND IT'S SO EASY TO DO."

SERENA WILLIAMS

When our days become very busy, our brains don't always get a chance to think through all that has happened. Then, at bedtime, our brains become overactive, processing everything and thinking about all the things we are worried about, which deprives us of much needed sleep. Spend two minutes on a "brain dump" by writing down all your worries on paper here so you don't have to think of them at bedtime.

_____

_____

_____

_____

_____

_____

_____

_____

_____

_____

_____

_____

_____

_____

_____

_____

_____

_____

After women have babies, they relate to people differently. You may find that you cannot carry on conversations in the same way or that you desire more or less time alone. How have your relationships changed since having a baby?

_____

_____

_____

_____

_____

_____

_____

_____

How are you feeling about these changes?

_____

_____

_____

_____

What would you like to be different?

_____

_____

_____

_____

_____

As we age, new pieces are added to our identity without us realizing it. By naming these pieces we honor them, create space for them, and acknowledge the effort they take. Brainstorm the roles that you play in a day and circle the relevant ones below. Add new ones, if desired.

Mother	Sister	Organizer
Bookkeeper	Employee	Counselor
Scheduler	Employer	Mediator
Lover	Housekeeper	Playmate
Friend	Chef	Disciplinarian
Partner	Meal planner	Teacher
Daughter	Event planner	Researcher

Your Priorities

If you could choose what aspects of your life to prioritize, what would those priorities be? Make a pie chart showing how you want to allocate your energy using the following categories (plus any others you wish to add):

    romance/partnership, job, leisure, friends, parenting/children, mental and physical wellness, social citizenship, family, spirituality, personal growth

Try to think about how much energy you want to dedicate to each category, rather than time. For instance, you might spend a great deal of energy on conversations with friends because it feels taxing for you, but it might not take up much time.

Sleep is a big predictor of mental wellness, and getting enough is a huge challenge as a new parent. Sleep deprivation can cause anxiety, depression, poor memory and, in extreme cases, hallucinations and delusions. Think about your past relationship to rest and sleep. How have you previously prioritized sleep?

How does sleep loss affect you?

How much sleep have you needed in the past in order to feel happy and healthy?

Getting Better Sleep

Getting enough sleep with a kiddo at home requires creativity, but it will get better over time. Brainstorm some ideas about how to get more or better sleep below. Circle any of the suggestions you'd like to consider trying yourself.

→   I will skip the first night-feeding and have my partner give a bottle so I get a bigger chunk of sleep.

→   When it's my partner's turn to get up with the baby, I'll wear earplugs and turn the monitor off.

→   We will hire a night nanny for one night.

→   I'll nap instead of doing chores when the baby sleeps.

→   Once a night, my partner can get the baby, bring them to me, and latch them on so I can stay mostly asleep.

→   We will do one bottle of formula a night.

→   We will hire a sleep consultant for help.

→   I will drop one commitment so that I have more time for rest

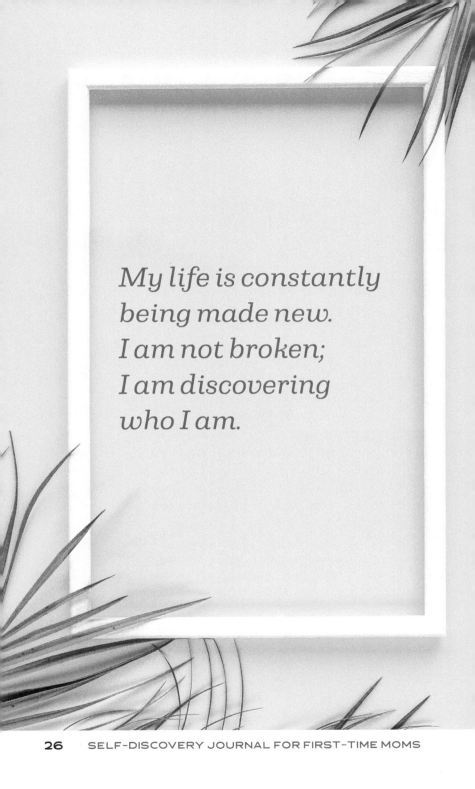

*My life is constantly
being made new.
I am not broken;
I am discovering
who I am.*

Take a moment to thank yourself for dedicating time and energy to this journey of self-discovery. You've put in a lot of work already! Write your future self a message about what you have learned about yourself so far. Specifically, recall things you have learned that have made you feel good or proud of who you are. Practice using kind and compassionate language as you write.

_____

_____

_____

_____

_____

_____

_____

_____

_____

_____

_____

_____

_____

_____

_____

_____

_____

"THE BOTTOM LINE
IS HAVING SOME
TIME TO RECONNECT
WITH OUR ESSENCE
[. . .] THAT INCREDIBLE
STRENGTH, WISDOM,
AND SENSE OF
WELL-BEING
THAT'S INSIDE US."

ARIANNA HUFFINGTON

EMBRACE YOUR EMOTIONAL SELF

Emotions are what our body uses to signal us about what we are experiencing. In motherhood, you may be overwhelmed by how quickly these signals change: from joy to grief, from love to loneliness, from calm to rage, from contentment to jealousy. Often, we have the idea that some emotions are "bad" or "negative," and we have learned to avoid them or push them down. This can take a toll over time.

When we view emotions as neutral pieces of information, we can allow them to come and go. Bringing awareness and acceptance to whatever thoughts and feelings we have in the moment lets them pass through us rather than becoming bottled up.

In this section, you will learn how to better understand your thoughts and feelings, identify your reactions to them, notice thinking patterns that cause you pain, and use practices to support you in your journey in embracing your emotional self.

We often have ideas about motherhood before we even think of having a baby. We see pictures of glowing new mothers on Instagram and it all looks so easy. The reality is that motherhood is all the things: heartwarming, crazy-making, messy, exhausting, fulfilling, incredible, and more. All of your feelings are valid just as they are. This is a space for you to practice letting yourself have all the feelings. Complete these sentences to create more space for every side of you.

I love it when _____

_____

I give myself permission to feel jealous of _____

_____

I feel bad that _____

_____

I feel happy when I _____

_____

I give myself permission to be happy about _____

_____

My favorite moment of being a mom is _____

_____

I hate it when my child _____

_____

I love it when my partner _____

_____

I give myself permission to be angry about _____

_____

When I look at myself in the mirror, I feel _____

I hate it when my partner _____

I feel most alone when _____

I feel loved when _____

I give myself permission to feel sad about _____

I know I am important when _____

The thing I hate most about being a parent is _____

When I became a parent, I was surprised that _____

I give myself permission to feel scared about _____

When I think about myself as a mom, I love that I _____

I feel joy when _____

_____

_____

_____

When you think back to the experience of your child being born or adopted into your home, what images, thoughts, or emotions come to mind? If you could go back and talk to that version of yourself, what would you tell her, knowing what you know now?

_____

_____

_____

_____

_____

_____

_____

_____

_____

_____

_____

_____

_____

_____

_____

_____

_____

_____

Emotions and actions sometimes get linked in our minds, but it's important to remember that emotions are just information our brain is giving us about a situation and are independent of action. List some emotions you experience that you consider "bad" or "negative."

_____

_____

_____

_____

_____

_____

_____

_____

What actions do you assume are paired with these emotions? Link them with the emotions you listed above. For example, often people think that being angry is "bad" because they may associate anger with someone yelling, giving them the silent treatment, or saying hurtful things.

_____

_____

_____

_____

_____

_____

_____

_____

When we dream, our brain has a chance to process events from our waking life and make sense of what we are feeling. What striking dreams have you had lately? Briefly describe one or more of them here.

_____

_____

_____

_____

_____

_____

_____

Now, of the dreams above, think of the one that makes you feel the most emotional when you reflect on it. Imagine it is a message that you are receiving from an inner part of yourself. What might this dream be telling you?

_____

_____

_____

_____

_____

_____

_____

Rituals are powerful traditions that we, as humans, use to provide meaning, feel grounded, and mark important moments. As a new mother, a daily ritual can help you leave behind what came before and create space for what comes next. This could be taking time to mindfully massage your favorite facial oil along your jawline, sinuses, and forehead each day; or it could simply mean reading a poem before you sleep each night. In the space below, identify one ritual you would like to practice daily. Keep it simple. (Remember: If you find that your ritual isn't serving you after a few days or weeks, change it to something else.)

Take a moment to think about how your parents handled emotions when you were growing up. Then think about how you wish to set an example for showing emotions as a parent. With these considerations in mind, answer the following questions.

How did your parents show their feelings, and what messages did they directly teach you about feelings?

_____

_____

_____

What feelings did they not show in front of you?

_____

_____

_____

How did your childhood affect how you experience emotions now?

_____

_____

_____

Is there anything you want to do differently as a parent?

_____

_____

_____

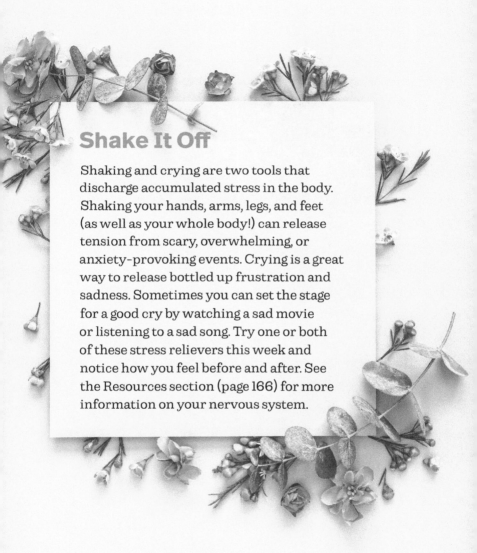

Shake It Off

Shaking and crying are two tools that discharge accumulated stress in the body. Shaking your hands, arms, legs, and feet (as well as your whole body!) can release tension from scary, overwhelming, or anxiety-provoking events. Crying is a great way to release bottled up frustration and sadness. Sometimes you can set the stage for a good cry by watching a sad movie or listening to a sad song. Try one or both of these stress relievers this week and notice how you feel before and after. See the Resources section (page 166) for more information on your nervous system.

What beliefs or preconceived notions do you have that stop you from fully enjoying motherhood? Beliefs such as, "Others should always come first," or, "I can't rest while others are working," might prevent you from getting your own needs met. Write down three beliefs and standards you hold yourself to that might prevent you from receiving self-care.

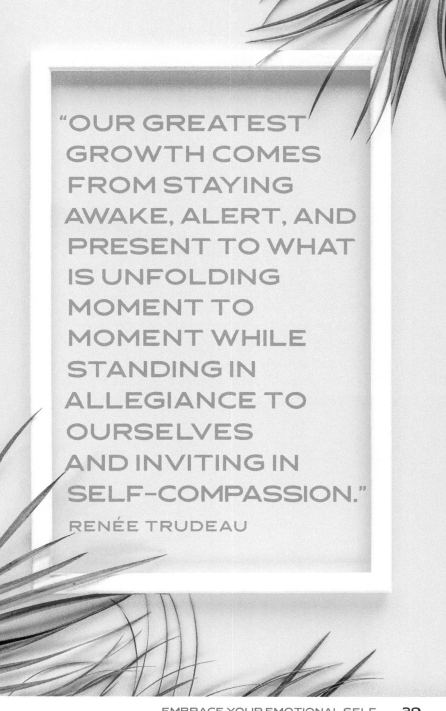

"OUR GREATEST GROWTH COMES FROM STAYING AWAKE, ALERT, AND PRESENT TO WHAT IS UNFOLDING MOMENT TO MOMENT WHILE STANDING IN ALLEGIANCE TO OURSELVES AND INVITING IN SELF-COMPASSION."

RENÉE TRUDEAU

Emotions are meant to flow through us: They build and crest like a wave and then disappear when left unobstructed. When we avoid feeling emotions, we "bottle them up," which can lead to unexpected outbursts of rage or irritation. In what ways do you avoid feeling emotions? List any emotions that you tend to "bottle up."

_____

_____

_____

_____

_____

Acknowledging an emotion allows it to flow through you. You can do this by naming it in the moment (e.g., "I'm feeling really mad and need to step away for a minute") or letting it move through your body when it is safe (e.g., crying or punching a pillow). Close your eyes and try to acknowledge any emotions you might have stored away. How do you feel afterwards?

_____

_____

_____

_____

_____

A Calming Tune

The vagus nerve connects our brain and our gut and is responsible for our "gut instinct." It is an important part of the parasympathetic nervous system that helps us relax. Humming, singing, and chanting activate the vagus nerve and our relaxation response; an added bonus is that singing and humming while holding your baby will relax both of you.

Choose a favorite tune, or select a mantra to repeat (see the Resources section on page 169 for ideas and tunes). Then practice singing, humming, or chanting it at times when you are already relaxed and also at times when you are stressed. Notice how you feel before and after.

Having a child often leads us to relive old hurts from our own childhood that took place at the age our child is currently. Take a moment to imagine yourself as a child. Create a full picture of yourself in your mind, including your age, what you would be wearing, and where you would be. As you imagine yourself, write down what this child most needs to hear in order to feel loved and safe.

I alone know my truth. I am loveable just as I am.

Emotions are generally paired with sensations in our body. Using the chart below, circle any sensations that you have felt in your body today or are feeling now. Notice what emotions you might be experiencing. Brainstorm what might have led to that emotion.

Emotion	Sensations in the Body	Possible Cause(s)
Anger	Clenched jaw Soreness around shoulder blades Tight buttocks, feet, or hands Tight eyes Tight neck muscles Headache	
Sadness	Lump or tightness in throat Tears Heaviness in limbs Sleepiness Heavy stomach Spine in a "c" shape or slumped posture Numbness	
Happiness	Whole-body lightness and buoyancy Smile on your lips Loose joints Upright posture Free-flowing movement	
Anxiety	Faster heart rate Stomachache or heartburn Stiff body with arms tight to body Fidgety movements that are small and rapid (e.g., leg swinging, tapping, jumping leg) Pulled in or tight stomach Overly tight pelvic floor Soft bowel movements or diarrhea Tingling	

What are ways that you calm and soothe yourself in the face of difficult emotions and experiences? Write down all the coping strategies you use (even the non-ideal ones, such as drinking or isolating). Put a star next to the ones you would like to do less of. Circle the ones you would like to do more of, or add more to your list that you would like to try doing in the future and circle those.

Self-compassion has been found to be strongly linked to experiencing happiness. Imagine yourself as a wise, warm, and kind mentor. Write a letter to yourself as a new mother, encouraging yourself on your journey. Offer words of love, warmth, and reassurance.

Try Some Yoga

Yoga nidra has been said to accomplish
in 40 minutes what three hours of sleep
provides for you. Try finding 40 minutes
in the coming day for a yoga nidra practice.
You will need a soft place to lie down (a
mattress or several yoga mats), a blanket,
something for covering your eyes (a wash-
cloth or eye pillow), and pillows to support
your body. Choose a practice from the
Resources section (page 169) to listen to.

Affirmations not only help us to think positively, but they also open and soften us so we are more likely to fulfill the affirmation itself. Write five positive affirmations you can turn to when you need a pick-me-up. You might draw on sayings from trusted mentors or friends, or make up phrases that speak to you, such as "May I feel confident."

"TIME IS PRECIOUS [TO MOMS], AND SO MANY OF US UNDERSTAND THE STRUGGLE TO SEEK BALANCE."

KAMALA HARRIS

We often end up comparing ourselves to the mothers we see on Pinterest, Facebook, and Instagram, even though we know that these mothers aren't "real" and show an idealized version of motherhood. Journal about your own experience as a social media–using mother. How do you feel when you are on social media? What do you want to change about your social media use?

_____

_____

_____

_____

_____

_____

_____

_____

_____

_____

_____

_____

_____

_____

_____

_____

_____

_____

Help From My Friends

Our friends can be great for helping us to see ourselves more accurately. Text at least five people and ask them to tell you one thing they love most about you. Put the responses on notecards or sticky notes that you can use as reminders of who you really are. You might put them by your bed to read every morning or stick them around the house.

Guilt is a common emotion among mothers because of the high standards women are taught to hold themselves to and the "we can do it all" story many are taught to believe. Write two or three things you feel guilty about. Check in with yourself to see if your guilt might be based on a perfectionistic or "we can do it all" standard. (If you aren't sure, this is a great time to "phone a friend" to get some fact-checking.)

Mother's intuition is a real thing, although we often find ourselves ignoring our gut instincts and instead doing what those in authority suggest. Many women experience this in conversations with health-care workers in particular. What causes you to doubt your gut? What are things you can tell yourself to help hold onto and trust your intuition?

Thoughts, behaviors, and emotions are intricately linked and often flow together, even though they are separate experiences. A harsh thought can lead us to feeling sad, while dancing or laughing with a friend can help lift a sad mood. Complete this chart by listing thoughts that often get "stuck" in your head and noting what emotions they get connected to. In the last two columns, put down a "friendly thought" or something a friend would tell you if they heard you say the negative thought out loud, and pick a behavior that might help lift the associated mood.

Thought	Emotion	Friendly Thought	Pick-Me-Up Behavior
Example: I'm so lazy, I can't even get the dishes done.	Sadness	No one stays on top of cleaning dishes with a young child at home.	Go for a walk outside and listen to a podcast.

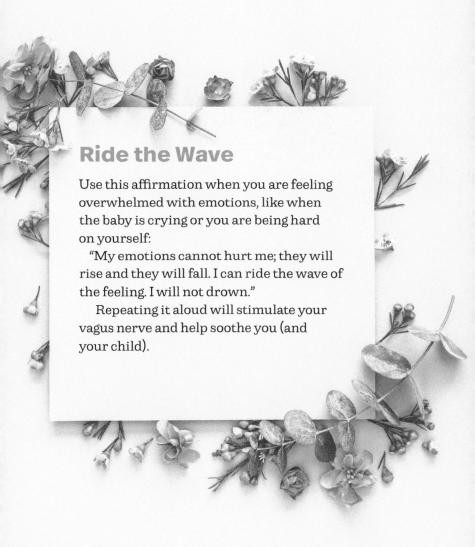

Ride the Wave

Use this affirmation when you are feeling overwhelmed with emotions, like when the baby is crying or you are being hard on yourself:

"My emotions cannot hurt me; they will rise and they will fall. I can ride the wave of the feeling. I will not drown."

Repeating it aloud will stimulate your vagus nerve and help soothe you (and your child).

"WE ARE ALWAYS PREGNANT WITH A TRUER VERSION OF OURSELVES."

MARIANNE WILLIAMSON

RECLAIM
YOUR IDENTITY

We spend so much of the early days of motherhood being one with our child, it can be challenging to remember that we exist as an individual. As our children begin to move away from us—sleeping separately, eating separately, crawling, walking—it can feel uncomfortable or even terrifying to let them separate.

This is true, in part, because we are left with a new self that we are not yet ready to be alone with. To help with this vital step of your journey, we will spend the next section helping you fall in love with who you are. We all rediscover ourselves at different life stages, but no change is so dramatic as becoming a mother. Fall in love with yourself in this new phase of life, so you can more boldly love those around you.

What is it like to think about being a separate person from your child? What do you like and resist about this idea? Are there ways that "mother" is taking up more space than is aligned with your values and goals? (Check in on your values from page 3 earlier in the journal.)

_____

_____

_____

_____

_____

_____

_____

_____

_____

_____

_____

_____

_____

_____

_____

_____

Women often have an internal critical voice telling them what they "should" and "shouldn't" do. Sometimes these stories help us stay safe, but more often, they become a burden that causes us to self-criticize. What are some stories you have about what you "should" be or do that make you feel less-than? For example, after having my first child, I thought that I "should" want to spend all my free time with her, and I felt guilty and told myself I was a "bad mom" because I didn't.

_____

_____

_____

_____

_____

_____

_____

Which "shoulds" do you want to let go of? What do you want to give yourself permission to feel?

_____

_____

_____

_____

_____

_____

_____

I step into my true self with love, strength, and patience.

An attitude of curiosity invites wonder and joy into your life. Nourishing your creative and curious side helps you find joy and pleasure amidst the humdrum of diapers, dishes, and bills. What are topics that you find interesting and would love to learn about?

_____

_____

_____

_____

_____

_____

Are there aspects of life you would like to focus on more?

_____

_____

_____

_____

_____

How would you like to integrate these interests into your life in a new way?

_____

_____

_____

_____

A simple trick to help you feel motivated is to give yourself a reward for doing hard things. Remember: Your definition of hard might need some adjusting at this stage of life. Even playing with a baby for 30 minutes after no sleep can feel next to impossible. Below are some ideas for ways to reward yourself, with space to write down a third for each category.

	Inexpensive Rewards	Special Rewards
Quick (instant to 30 minutes)	1. Heat a neck-wrap and sit on your bed with music playing 2. Enjoy your favorite snack or treat instead of doing chores. 3.	1. Order takeout from a nearby restaurant you love 2. Buy yourself a present to pamper yourself 3.
Short (30 minutes to 1 hour)	1. Take a bath and watch your favorite show 2. Ask a friend to watch your kid for an hour 3.	1. Hire a sitter and enjoy coffee and a book undisturbed 2. Get a chair massage at a drop-in spot 3.
Long (half a day or more)	1. Go on a hike on a trail you love 2. Spend an afternoon at a friend's house without your child 3.	1. Book a night away from everyone 2. Take a workshop on a topic you've been interested in 3.

How we spend our time changes dramatically after having a baby. You may find that you have to say "no" to social activities more often because you don't have the same amount of energy that you had before. If you are sensitive to disappointing people, it might be hard to put your own needs first. Write about what you want to make more time for in your schedule. Then make a list of what you want to say "no" to more often.

The addition of a child to your house has likely influenced how you feel about your body, whether you gave birth, adopted, or otherwise. Spend some time reflecting on and writing down how you feel about your new mother-body. Try to touch on many feelings, no matter how slight they seem.

_____

_____

_____

_____

_____

_____

_____

_____

_____

_____

_____

_____

_____

_____

_____

_____

_____

_____

Share Your Goals

When we say things aloud, we bring a reality to them that we experience differently from when we just hold them in our own mind. Consider what goals you have for the next few years (check in on the goals from earlier on page 11), then talk them through with your partner or a loved one. Focus on naming what is important to you and how these goals make you feel. Afterward, reflect on what it was like to share them. How did sharing them with someone affect how you feel about them?

The term "mama bear" often describes the fierce strength of a mother. Once women have a baby, they often become aware of a new power that they weren't aware of before. Sometimes this feeling manifests immediately; other times it might not show up until your child is older. What surprises you about the strength of motherhood? What animal describes this part of you?

Sometimes we get in the habit of saying "yes" to things that please others and "no" to opportunities for caring for ourselves. Reflect on what you have said "yes" and "no" to lately. Is there anything you want to do differently going forward?

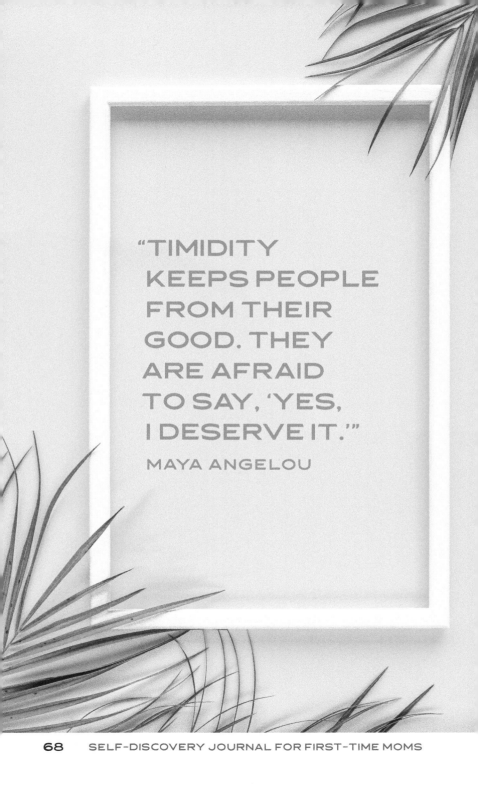

"TIMIDITY KEEPS PEOPLE FROM THEIR GOOD. THEY ARE AFRAID TO SAY, 'YES, I DESERVE IT.'"

MAYA ANGELOU

Women are often raised to "keep the peace" in the world. Unfortunately, sometimes we take this too far and lose our own voices so that others won't experience sadness, anger, or disappointment. Write about how you have avoided doing what is good for you in order to keep the peace. What feelings do you try to "protect" others from? How does this prevent you from fully stepping into yourself?

_____

_____

_____

_____

_____

_____

_____

Now, think of a time you've not shared your emotional experience in order to "protect" someone else. Write down one or more ways you could have shared that feeling appropriately.

_____

_____

_____

_____

_____

_____

_____

_____

Welcoming Change

Having a child is like driving through the neighborhood but taking a new path every day; your days are both insanely repetitive and wildly unpredictable. Challenge yourself to embrace some unpredictability in your life by inviting it in. Take a different route to the store. When going on a walk, go in the opposite direction you would normally go. Play a different type of music than you would normally listen to. By controlling our exposure to unpredictable outcomes, we teach our brains flexibility and feel less anxious when presented with novelty.

The emotional load that women carry can create a sense of constant tension and burden. What are five things on your to-do list that are bothering you because they aren't done?

_____

_____

_____

_____

_____

_____

_____

Now consider what will realistically happen if you don't do them. What is one task that you can decide not to do? What is one task that you can ask someone else to do?

_____

_____

_____

_____

_____

_____

_____

_____

_____

"SOMETIMES IT FEELS LIKE IF WE STOP WORKING, THE FLOOR IS GOING TO FALL OUT FROM UNDER EVERYONE BECAUSE WE HOLD EVERYTHING UP. AND MY FRIEND, THAT IS THE EPITOME OF ARROGANCE."

GENEVIEVE SAENZ

When we are grounded, the "I can do it better" attitude demonstrates our confidence and our skills. When we feel panicky, anxious, or fearful, we sometimes use "I can do it better" to get control over a situation. Write about a time that you have said or thought, "I can do it better," recently. Did this attitude give you control when you felt the lack of it, and did it come from feeling grounded and confident? How does an "I can do it better" attitude keep you stuck doing an unfair share of tasks?

_____

_____

_____

_____

_____

_____

_____

_____

_____

_____

_____

_____

_____

_____

_____

_____

Vision Board

A vision board captures your dreams, desires, plans, and goals. Having a visual reminder in front of you helps you stay on track, feel inspired, and stay connected to yourself. To create one, gather a large sheet of paper (ideally something stiff like cardstock, but anything will do); tape or glue; magazines or printed images from the internet; markers (permanent are great for writing on glossy paper); and stickers or other decorative items. Cut out or choose words or images that inspire you or relate to your goals (check in on the goals you identified on page 11) and arrange them on the large paper. Remember, there's no need to make it "pretty" or "do it right." Make sure you look at your board daily for inspiration.

You are not your mother, whether you want to be or fear that you will be. Write about both the fears you have of being your mother (or any other caretaker), as well as the things you admire about her. Write down the qualities you are proud of in yourself that might be different from those of your mother, as well as those you inherited from her.

Being a first-time parent means accepting that you are a new learner at this task and may need help at times. If you had a parenting expert in front of you, what is one thing you would tell them you are proud of about your parenting? What is one thing that you need help with?

_____

_____

_____

_____

_____

_____

_____

_____

_____

_____

_____

_____

_____

_____

_____

_____

Our hobbies change as we move through the different phases of our lives. You might not be able to spend a whole afternoon painting or gardening right now the way you did just a year ago. That doesn't mean that you don't get to enjoy yourself. What are hobbies that you've had in the past that you've loved? How could you adjust your life to fit in one of those hobbies now?

_____

_____

_____

_____

_____

_____

_____

_____

_____

_____

_____

_____

_____

_____

_____

_____

_____

_____

There is a YOLO-style pressure to "do it all" as a mother. Actually, you don't have to do it all, nor can you as a human being. For now, you might have to group your goals based on the life stage of your child. Complete the chart below with your goals, and remember that you have a whole life to accomplish them.

INFANCY

Your child is taking longer naps and not yet walking, which might make it easier for you to talk with friends or do bite-sized tasks.

MY GOALS: _____
_____
_____
_____

TODDLERHOOD

This is one of the hardest times for mothers in which to get things done: Toddlers don't want to sit still, they crave attention, and they have tantrums when confronted with limits. If you are stressed about reaching goals, remember that it won't be like this forever and offer yourself compassion through this challenging time.

MY GOALS: _____
_____
_____
_____

ELEMENTARY

Finally! Your child will sit and do things alone. Or can leave the house alone! This is your chance to add things to your plate without relying on childcare as much.

MY GOALS: _____
_____
_____
_____

LATE ELEMENTARY/MIDDLE SCHOOL

With the ability to leave your child home alone, your whole world is reopening. You can go to a yoga class or stop for coffee without finding a sitter. Or (gasp) go on a weekend day-date with your partner! What would you like to focus on in this stage?

MY GOALS: _____
_____
_____
_____
_____

HIGH SCHOOL

Your kid might not even want to see you during this stage and, ironically, you could be the one trying to get their attention. Do you want to be more available to your kid as they get ready to launch into the world, or is this your chance to fill your plate, now that you can?

MY GOALS: _____
_____
_____
_____
_____

ADULTHOOD

Empty nest! Okay, you might not be able to even think this far. But it's worth remembering that there will be a time in your life when you will not have any dependents and you'll be able to fully embrace your own needs again.

MY GOALS: _____
_____
_____
_____
_____

Motherhood can highlight detrimental perfectionism that you might have managed before you had kids. In the past, you might have been close enough to perfection that your performance wasn't a problem. Now, however, you might be feeling extreme anxiety when the dishes aren't done or the laundry isn't folded, and it's making it hard to rest or nap; or you cannot even start because you know things won't be perfect. How do you relate to being a perfectionist? How are perfectionistic tendencies setting you up for unrealistic expectations for yourself?

_____

_____

_____

_____

_____

_____

_____

_____

_____

_____

_____

_____

_____

_____

What is most difficult for you at your child's current stage? Consider the idea of lowering your expectations or asking for help in regard to these struggles. What could you do to make life easier? What expectations might you need to change to be more realistic?

Pay attention when you hear a story in your head like, "I don't want to be a bother," or, "Others should come first." These stories prevent you from taking care of yourself. They also model for your kids that women should put themselves low on the priority list. What behavior do you want to model for your children when it comes to prioritizing yourself and loving yourself?

Put Your Comfort First

Many of us have learned we should "just do Kegels" to fix or prevent pelvic floor problems. However, it's come to light that many women either do Kegels wrong or have overly tight muscles that are actually causing the problem. Put a check mark by any issues you may be experiencing. If you've checked one or more boxes and feel that any of these are affecting your quality of life, you may benefit from working with a pelvic-floor physical therapist. These are fixable issues, and you don't deserve to be uncomfortable.

- ☐ Urinary leakage while moving, laughing, coughing, or jumping

- ☐ Unexpected bowel release

- ☐ Leakage of wind

- ☐ Constipation

- ☐ Frequently using the toilet

- ☐ Getting up at night to use the toilet enough times that it's significantly interrupting your sleep

- ☐ A feeling that you cannot totally empty your bladder

- ☐ A feeling of heaviness, weight, or bulging from the vagina

- ☐ Pain in your pelvic region during any activity

- ☐ Pain during sex or tampon use

- ☐ Pain in the pelvis

- ☐ Reduced sensation in the vaginal area

"WE ARRIVED ON THIS PLANET AS LOVE. OUR ORIGINAL RELATIONSHIP TO OUR OWN BODIES AND TO THE BODIES OF OTHERS WAS LOVE. YOU'VE NEVER SEEN A TODDLER WHO IS LIKE, 'I JUST REALLY HATE MY THIGHS.'"

SONYA RENEE TAYLOR

RECONNECT
WITH YOUR
BODY

Women are dynamic, powerful creatures. We have amazing creativity, passion, love, and drive. Unfortunately, many of us are out of touch with this inner power. Instead, we have been taught to focus on what we "should" have: smooth skin, skinny thighs, a flat belly, curves (but not too many) . . . I could go on.

We forget that these "shoulds" are completely made up and often created to maintain a power hierarchy. The truth is that women hold incredible power within, both in their spirits and in their bodies. As a woman, your body is alluring and comforting; strong and soft; powerful and life-creating.

In this section, I will challenge you to honor your feminine self in all its beauty by practicing how to give your body nourishment, pleasure, and gratitude for all that it does for you.

Spend time being tender with yourself. Allow yourself space to write about ways you have experienced judgment about your body, ranging from ableism to fat phobia to sexism. At the end of your journaling, write the following affirmation three times: "I am whole just as I am. I am worthy of love."

_____

_____

_____

_____

_____

_____

_____

_____

_____

_____

_____

_____

_____

_____

_____

_____

_____

_____

_____

_____

We are all more than just our bodies, and we are also intimately tied to how our bodies are cared for. The amount of sleep, quality of food, and the way we move all affect how we think and feel, because of the body-brain connection. Spend some time writing a love letter to your body for all it has done for you. What would you want to say to show your appreciation?

Starting the Day

Give yourself permission to start your day with self-care as the focus, but in a realistic, mama-friendly way. Choose three stretches—ideally ones that you can do while still in bed! A simple twist or knees-to-chest stretch is easy to do while lying under the covers. Try to do your stretches every morning this week before you start your day. Check out the Resources section (page 166) for ideas.

Most cultures have a day of rest as part of their rhythm of life, and for good reason. From a biological standpoint, our bodies need to be in a rested state in order to do functions such as digestion, memory consolidation, energy creation, and excretion of toxins. From a spiritual standpoint, rest allows us to see and acknowledge beauty and live with joy. Create a plan to add rest into your week.

When you were growing up, your parents may not have taught you much about your body and how it works. You might have learned to be ashamed of menstruation, your body's changes, or your different needs as your hormones change during the month. Reflect on what you were taught about menstruation and women's mood changes. Consider messages you received from family, friends, the opposite gender, and media. How are they different from reality?

Honor Your Body

Practice showing respect and appreciation for the cycle your body undergoes by honoring your different needs throughout the month. Once you understand the cycle of your hormones, you will be able to predict your moods, energy levels, and needs more accurately. Spend a few minutes reading about menstruation, hormones, and mood. If you are a menstruating woman, download an app like Hormonology or print their monthly chart that gives you regular notifications about what to expect. See the Resources section (page 166) for ideas.

The phrase "working out" usually implies a goal to make your body look a certain way, as opposed to focusing on being strong or healthy. If you used the phrase "caring for myself" or even "being active" instead of "working out," how would that change the meaning and your motivation? Spend a few minutes journaling on this idea.

A Ritual to Reflect

Practice a ritual to mark the luteal halfway point of your cycle or, if you are a non-menstruating mother, use the new moon as a time-point. This marks a time of turning inward, quiet, and introspection to prepare for the outward energy of the full moon. This is also a time to focus on routine tasks and avoid new events. Use this ritual (or create your own) as a reminder to shift your focus, slow down, and reflect on what you need. Set a reminder on your phone so you remember!

1. Opening of ritual: Light a candle, ring a bell, and state your intention.

2. Gratitude: Say a prayer or state gratitude, such as "I am grateful for this body that carries me, for taking this time to love myself, and for the wise women guiding me."

3. Affirmation: "I honor all women by listening to my inner truth and following my wisdom."

4. Honoring your body: Spend some time stretching and self-massaging any tense muscles you can reach.

5. Reflection: Spend a moment writing down what you need in the next week.

6. Closing of ritual: Blow out the candle, ring a bell, and say a prayer or recite an affirming statement.

Being "touched out," a sensation of feeling averse to being touched, is a frequent complaint of mothers of young children. Feeling this way indicates that your nervous system is overwhelmed and you need to prioritize caring for yourself and your body. Write down things that will help you when you are feeling "touched out." Spend a few moments identifying the warning signs that indicate you are getting closer to being "touched out" so you can head off the experience before you are irritated and overwhelmed.

Many women have been conditioned to think that their bodies need to fit their clothes and not the other way around. Where have you learned that your body should be a certain size or shape? What comes up when you think about your body changing size and shape over the course of your lifetime? What prevents you from buying clothes that fit your current body?

_____

_____

_____

_____

_____

_____

_____

_____

_____

_____

_____

_____

_____

_____

_____

_____

_____

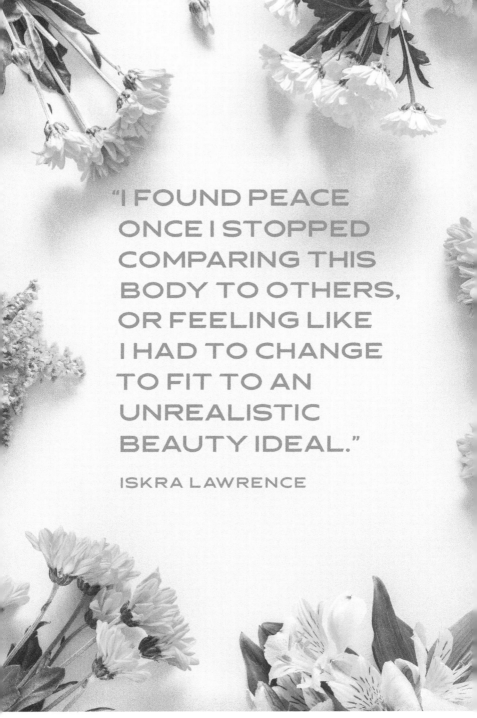

"I FOUND PEACE
ONCE I STOPPED
COMPARING THIS
BODY TO OTHERS,
OR FEELING LIKE
I HAD TO CHANGE
TO FIT TO AN
UNREALISTIC
BEAUTY IDEAL."

ISKRA LAWRENCE

Taking Up Space

Women are often taught to be smaller in life: Be shorter than men; be thin; step out of the way; don't interrupt; be nice always. Think about the ways you expect yourself to be smaller or out of the way. Spend a week practicing taking up space: Wear clothes that fit and make you feel good; expect others to move out of your way when you walk; smile only if you feel like it. Notice how it feels to be in your body this way.

Our children learn about their bodies from us, just as we did from our families. Luckily, we can stop any negative generational messages when we give them mindful attention. What messages did you hear about bodies when you were growing up?

_____

_____

_____

_____

What are comments you make aloud now that might influence how your child feels about their body?

_____

_____

_____

_____

What would you like to do differently?

_____

_____

_____

_____

This body is strong and powerful. I can live a happy, healthy, complete life just as I am.

Having a place of comfort to return to in our imagination can help with managing stress, anxiety, and sadness. Describe a place in which you feel safe and loved, whether real or imagined. Make sure you use all the senses in your description: how it smells, what tastes there are, what it feels like, what you see, and what you hear. This place is a space you can return to in your mind whenever you need to feel comfort.

_____

_____

_____

_____

_____

_____

_____

_____

_____

_____

_____

_____

_____

_____

_____

_____

_____

We spend so much time in survival mode when we are with our kids, we are often wildly out of touch with the idea of experiencing pleasure. Write about how you receive pleasure. Is it through touch, taste, music? What pleasure do you want to add more of to your life? What stops you from doing so and how can you overcome those obstacles?

Just Dance

Dance is a powerful way to channel emotions and release them from being stored in your muscles. Put on music that reflects the mood you are in and let yourself move to the music. No one is watching (except the baby . . .). Allow yourself to feel the emotion in the music. Match your body's movement to the energy and mood in the music. Try this at other times throughout the week as a way to release your emotions from your body.

Think about people you know and those you follow on social media. Write down who makes you feel good about your body and who prompts thoughts that create judgment about yourself.

_____

_____

_____

_____

_____

_____

_____

_____

What might you need to change about whom you are exposed to? How can you protect yourself from their comments?

_____

_____

_____

_____

_____

_____

_____

_____

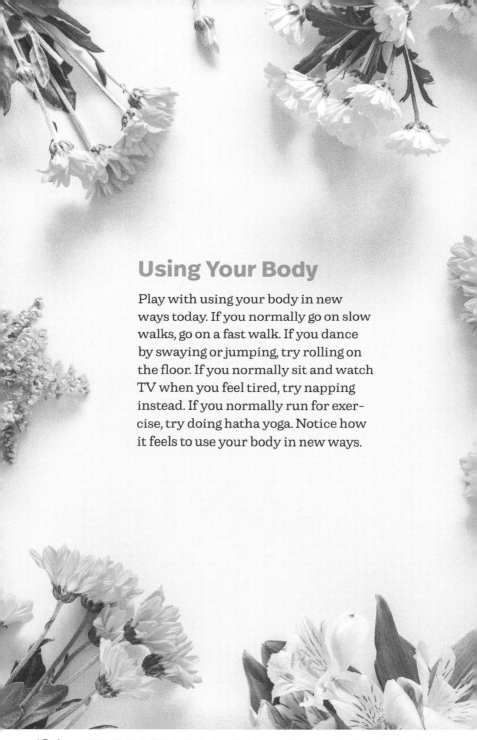

Using Your Body

Play with using your body in new
ways today. If you normally go on slow
walks, go on a fast walk. If you dance
by swaying or jumping, try rolling on
the floor. If you normally sit and watch
TV when you feel tired, try napping
instead. If you normally run for exercise, try doing hatha yoga. Notice how
it feels to use your body in new ways.

Many people suffer from insomnia and sleep problems. Create a restful bedtime routine for yourself using the prompts below. Circle ideas you'd like to use and add your own! Remember to turn screens off one hour before bed (looking at a screen doesn't allow your brain to transition to restful brainwaves even though your body is still). Make sure your routine starts at least 30 minutes before you want to be asleep.

1. Create a relaxation trigger:
   → Light a candle
   → Start an essential oil diffuser (use the same scent or similar scents each night)
   → Play soothing music
2. Prepare your body:
   → Brush teeth, wash face, etc.
   → Massage your jaw and your temples
   → Rub lotion on your feet
3. Prepare your mind:
   → Say a prayer
   → Repeat an affirmation
   → Use a mantra (see the Resources section on page 169 for ideas)
   → Practice breath work, like the square breath (see the Resources section on page 168 for ideas)
4. Create space for transition:
   → Read
   → Listen to an audiobook
   → Listen to a meditation

If you are getting distracted by worries, consider keeping a "worry notebook" by the bed that you can use to jot down your anxieties or "to-dos" to get them out of your head so you can relax.

_____

_____

_____

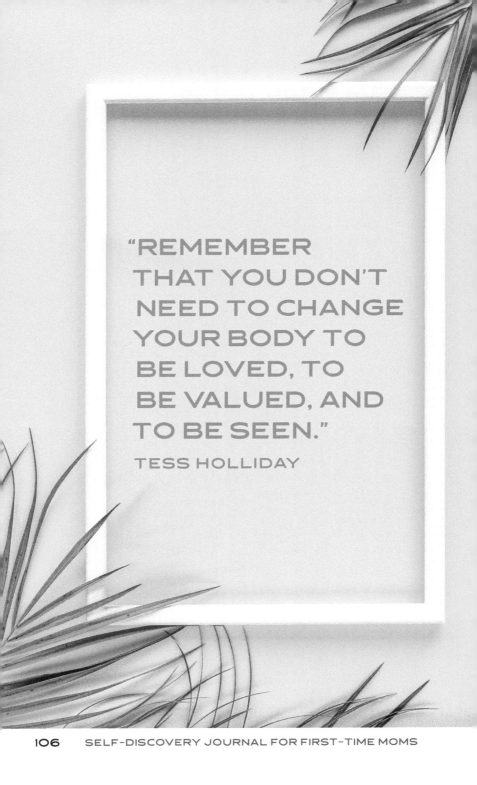

"REMEMBER
THAT YOU DON'T
NEED TO CHANGE
YOUR BODY TO
BE LOVED, TO
BE VALUED, AND
TO BE SEEN."

TESS HOLLIDAY

Mindful Eating

Mothers are known for unconsciously eating off their kids' plates for a reason: Eating on the run is a real thing. This week, try out a mindful eating exercise to help you tune into the pleasure and enjoyment you can get from eating. It doesn't have to be a full meal; just choose a snack or a treat you can enjoy if you're short on time. Several options for mindful eating meditations are in the Resources section (page 168).

After having a baby, you may relate to your sexual self differently due to bodily scarring, trauma, breastfeeding, or other changes. Journal about how you think of yourself as a sexual being. How has that changed since becoming a mother? What resistance do you have to thinking of yourself as sexual?

_____

_____

_____

_____

_____

_____

_____

_____

_____

_____

_____

_____

_____

_____

_____

_____

_____

_____

_____

Sex is much more than penetration, although we tend to focus on that, and specifically on male climax. But to feel sexual after having a baby, you might need penetrative sex to be "off the table" so you have permission to flirt, touch, and relax without feeling obligated to "finish the job." Spend time with the questions below and explore your desires and needs. How were you raised to think about sex?

_____

_____

_____

What kind of non-penetrative sexual touch and acts do you enjoy currently?

_____

_____

What prevents you from being sexually intimate with your partner right now?

_____

_____

_____

How do you feel about communicating your sexual needs to your partner or voicing them for yourself?

_____

_____

_____

Talking about sex can sometimes be easier outside of actual intimacy. What would you want to tell your partner about your needs? Include a time that would be best for you to have this conversation. Need help starting the conversation? Check out the Resources section (page 170) for ideas.

Congratulations: You've covered so much in this section! Take a moment to reflect on what you have learned about your body. What would you like to remember going forward?

_____

_____

_____

_____

_____

_____

_____

_____

What would you like to write to "future you" who may come back and read this?

_____

_____

_____

_____

_____

_____

_____

_____

"BUT THE BEST GIFT ANYONE CAN GIVE, I BELIEVE, IS THE GIFT OF SHARING THEMSELVES."

OPRAH

REACH OUTSIDE OF YOURSELF

Humans are designed to be social animals; the need for community is built into our bodies and brains. Too often our busy lives cause us to lean hard on social media for community instead of taking time to share space with people or connect in a meaningful way.

What we know from research is that close relationships with others, connection to community, and being hugged and touched by others protect us from depression and anxiety. While being seen can be scary, it is incredibly important to your health and wellness.

In this section, we will delve into the outer world and explore how you can learn to love yourself and step more fully into your life by stepping outside your door.

Our feelings about community are shaped by our early life experiences. Maybe you felt ostracized in one community. Maybe you felt held and loved deeply in another. Reflect below on what community means to you. What are negative associations that you've had with "community"? What are positive associations you would like to keep and develop that you've experienced or observed?

_____

_____

_____

_____

_____

_____

_____

_____

_____

_____

_____

_____

_____

_____

_____

_____

We often move through our social circles without recognizing where we fit, where we feel comfortable, or whom we belong to. Are you an active part of one or more communities? Write them down.

_____

_____

_____

_____

Which of these communities fill you up and which would you like to transition away from?

_____

_____

_____

_____

What communities are you part of that you haven't participated in much since you've been a new mom? How might you like that to change?

_____

_____

_____

_____

_____

Because social groups tend to be centered around the activities of our children, as moms we find ourselves around people of our own generation. This means we can miss out on the beautiful benefits younger and older people can offer us. Take a moment to reflect on how your friendships are (or aren't) cross-generational. Write down ways you could connect with people outside of your peer group.

_____

_____

_____

_____

_____

_____

_____

_____

_____

_____

_____

_____

_____

_____

_____

You might have a lovely support system around you and not even know it. Spend time exploring your feelings about your neighbors. What gets in the way of creating relationships with those that live around you? Is there one person you'd like to know better? What would it be like to invite them over for coffee or see if they want to meet for a front-yard hangout?

Try out one new community in the coming month. It could be a music class, a community of faith, or a social club. (If possible, avoid online communities, because it is hard to reap the same benefits as in-person relationships.) Write down a few ideas here, and circle one community you'd like to prioritize. Go ahead and set it up now, before you get distracted.

_____

_____

_____

_____

_____

_____

_____

_____

_____

_____

_____

_____

_____

_____

_____

_____

What role does helping others play in your life? Explore how being a "helper" influences how you feel about yourself. Remember that being a helper might look different with a young child at this life stage. What are new ways you can help, even if your schedule and energy have changed drastically?

_____

_____

_____

_____

_____

_____

_____

_____

_____

_____

_____

_____

_____

_____

_____

_____

Part of reaching outside of yourself and truly understanding who you are is involving yourself in settings and with people who are not like you. Take a moment to reflect on your interactions with people of a similar background, faith, or politics. What gets in the way of you reaching out to different groups? What is one way you can stretch yourself in the next month to step out of your bubble?

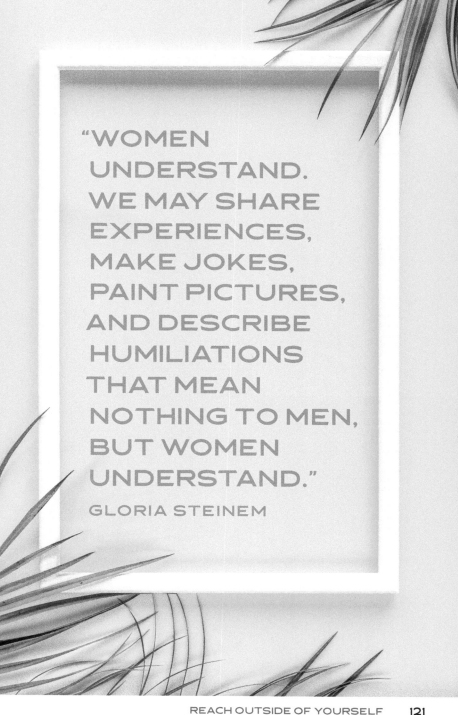

"WOMEN UNDERSTAND. WE MAY SHARE EXPERIENCES, MAKE JOKES, PAINT PICTURES, AND DESCRIBE HUMILIATIONS THAT MEAN NOTHING TO MEN, BUT WOMEN UNDERSTAND."

GLORIA STEINEM

Does it ever feel as if making mom friends is kind of like dating? There's that awkward, "Could I get your number," moment at the swing set and the anxiety of wondering how they feel about you. Mom dating isn't easy, but it must be done to make new friends. Is there someone you've seen that you'd like to know better? Create a plan to reach out to them to set up a "first date."

_____

_____

_____

_____

_____

_____

_____

_____

_____

_____

_____

_____

_____

_____

_____

_____

Being friends with other mothers is incredibly helpful in normalizing typically hard experiences and avoiding the "Facebook effect" of assuming everyone has their life together. But where do these moms hang out anyway? Ever feel as if you don't even know where to start? Brainstorm places where you could create some connections. Below are some ideas to get you started.

→ Day care
→ Mother's-day-out programs
→ Toddler music class
→ Mommy-and-me yoga class
→ Park playground
→ Child-friendly coffee shop

In the movies, there's the broody character who mutters, "Someday I'll call on you to pay back this favor." In real life, moms feel pressure to return favors as soon as they receive one. If you gave yourself permission to think of favors as being paid back over a lifetime, would you ask for help more often? How can you allow yourself to accept help even when you can't give it back right away?

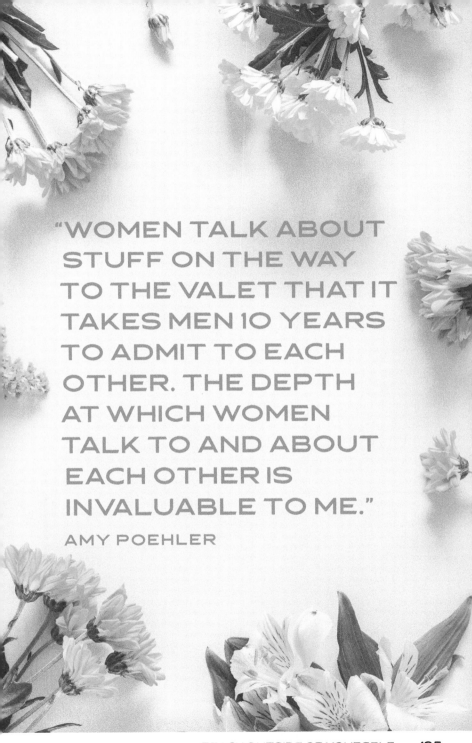

"WOMEN TALK ABOUT STUFF ON THE WAY TO THE VALET THAT IT TAKES MEN 10 YEARS TO ADMIT TO EACH OTHER. THE DEPTH AT WHICH WOMEN TALK TO AND ABOUT EACH OTHER IS INVALUABLE TO ME."

AMY POEHLER

Volunteering can be a fulfilling and meaningful way to connect with your community.
What strengths do you bring to the world
that you'd want to share by volunteering? Take
15 minutes to research volunteer activities in your area or
those you can do remotely that would be interesting and take
advantage of your strengths.

Play is a way to connect more deeply with your spiritual side, tap into your creative self, and show love to yourself. What are ways that you play alone and with other adults? What are new ways you'd like to add play into your life? Here are some ideas to get you started.

→ Dance
→ Play a board game with friends
→ Collect cool rocks
→ Fingerpaint
→ Sing karaoke with friends
→ Do a fun craft project
→ Have a water fight
→ Go puddle jumping

Write down your own ideas below.

_____

_____

_____

_____

_____

_____

_____

_____

_____

_____

_____

_____

_____

_____

Now that you've had a child, you might feel more distinctly that you have your "own" family that is separate from your parents, siblings, or other relatives. What does "family" mean to you? Think about the needs of your own family and those of your extended family. Journal about what role you'd like to have with your extended family now that you prioritize and care for a family of your own.

_____

_____

_____

_____

_____

_____

_____

_____

_____

_____

_____

_____

_____

_____

_____

_____

_____

Staying In Touch

Friendships take work, just like romantic relationships. It can often be challenging to maintain these connections when you have a new baby. Since everyone feels love differently, take a moment to think about what you can do this month to show one or two friends that you care. Make a plan now so you can intentionally connect with them. You might order a book and have it shipped to them, send them a postcard telling them what you love about them, or schedule a coffee date.

Relationships help us more accurately see ourselves. When we don't engage in friendships, we end up creating unfair comparisons of ourselves to celebrities or shiny Instagram moms. When we do this, we rarely imagine that we compare well. Journal about the people who see you for who you are. Who are they and what do they tell you they see? How would you benefit from spending more time with these people?

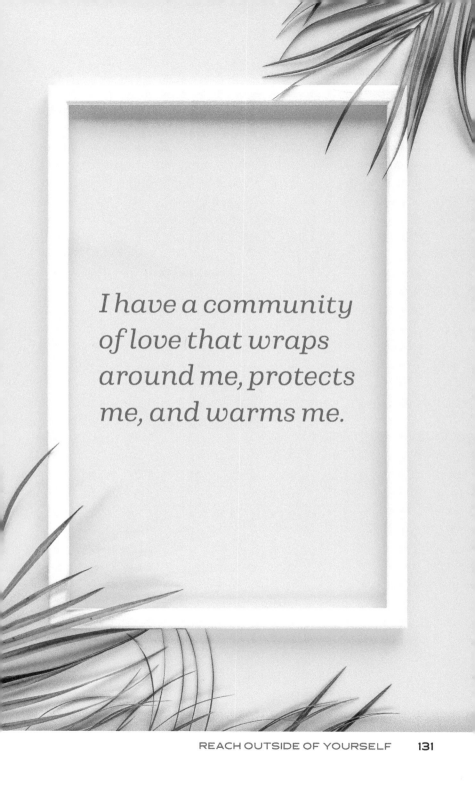

*I have a community
of love that wraps
around me, protects
me, and warms me.*

Sometimes we lose sight of communities we are part of when we become a family and need to juggle our new identity. You might have lost the queer side of yourself when you married a cis man. You might have stopped going to church after having a newborn. You might hang out with childless girlfriends less. Reflect on any losses in your community connections that you have experienced. Is there anything you would like to do differently?

Letter writing is a sweet way to connect with others in our lives. This week, send a letter to someone you care about. Limit it to one page (or even a postcard) so that you don't get overwhelmed by the task. What would you want them to know about your life and how you feel about them?

_____

_____

_____

_____

_____

_____

_____

_____

_____

_____

_____

_____

_____

_____

_____

_____

_____

_____

_____

Connect with your creativity by writing a poem. First, follow these prompts.

Name a person in your life:

_____

Name a song that makes you think of them:

_____

Write two sentences about a time they showed you love:

_____

_____

Name a movie or book that best describes them:

_____

Write down how they make you feel:

_____

_____

_____

Write down how you feel towards them:

_____

_____

_____

_____

Take these phrases and turn them into a poem.
Do this for as many people as you'd like.

We play different roles in the communities in our lives. Some-times we participate and other times we lead; sometimes we are the organizers and sometimes we are the advocates. Reflect on how you show up in communities around you. Are there ways you would benefit from trying out different roles? Are there places you can more fully step into yourself?

_____

_____

_____

_____

_____

_____

_____

_____

_____

_____

_____

_____

_____

_____

_____

_____

Take a moment to look back on your reflections and insights in this section. Notice what rings true, and what no longer resonates as it did when you wrote it. Give yourself permission to change your views and needs in this moment. List five points below that feel particularly relevant and important to you.

_____

_____

_____

_____

_____

_____

_____

_____

_____

_____

_____

_____

_____

_____

_____

_____

_____

_____

"I CAN ASSURE YOU
THAT WHEN I LOOK
BACK OVER MY LIFE,
"THIN" AND "RICH"
WILL BE TWO OF
THE LAST THINGS I
REALLY CARE ABOUT.
LOVING-KINDNESS,
AS BUDDHISM
CALLS IT, THAT'S
WHAT MATTERS."

ANNA QUINDLEN

THE PATH FORWARD

So far in this journal, you've done work exploring who you are, what is important to you, and how you want to show up in this world. This last section is focused on bringing it all together with intention so that you have resources to draw on as you move forward.

As you've learned through our work together, your identity is shifting and changing as you age and experience new aspects of life. While at times it may feel unsettling to be in a place that feels different and new, you were never meant to stay just one thing. You are an amazing being with a brightness within that will exist with you no matter what your life looks like, how you live it, or whom you live it with. Over the following pages you will review and reflect on what you've learned to enable your inner light to shine!

Rest creates a powerful space in which to listen to yourself. To enter this space, all you need to do is to slow down. Maybe that means setting aside your phone and just watching your child or the birds outside the window. Maybe that means lying down and breathing into your belly. What are ways that you've learned to rest through this journal's activities and practices?

_____

_____

_____

_____

_____

_____

_____

_____

_____

_____

_____

_____

_____

_____

_____

Loving Awareness

You can use your inner brightness to observe yourself and your life with love and compassion just as you are. We can use that observer-self to help us make intentional decisions, recognize our feelings before we act on them, and move forward in life with purpose. Choose one of the mindfulness practices in the Resources section (page 168) to develop your observing self. Consider downloading an app like Headspace, Calm, or Buddhify to make this an ongoing practice.

There is no "right way" to live life and be a mom, despite what that huge self-help and parenting section in the bookstore might indicate. What have you learned about how you latch onto ideas about "doing it right" or "getting it perfect"? What do you want to tell yourself in the future when those thoughts pop up?

Women have a powerful inner voice that guides us if we learn to listen to it. What have you learned about your intuition? How can your inner voice guide you in your life moving forward? At what times has listening to your intuition benefited you?

Draw the different identities you have that are a part of you. You can represent them however you like—as words, characters, animals, or images. When you are finished, take a moment to reflect on what your drawing teaches you about your identities. Which are bigger and which are smaller? Which were easy to identify and which were harder? What other things do you notice about your drawing?

"MY FULLEST
CONCENTRATION
OF ENERGY IS
AVAILABLE TO
ME ONLY WHEN
I INTEGRATE
ALL THE PARTS
OF WHO I AM."

AUDRE LORDE

Rediscovering yourself as time goes on will take intentionality because our society isn't set up to encourage taking time for introspection. How would you like to integrate time for turning inward going forward? What have you learned about this process and what works for you?

_____

_____

_____

_____

_____

_____

_____

_____

_____

_____

_____

_____

_____

_____

_____

_____

_____

_____

Planning "Me Time"

Sit down with any relevant planners (including people, if necessary) and schedule out time for rest, renewal, and self-discovery throughout the next six months. Block off these times as nonnegotiable days or hours you will take off from family life (and work) to tune into your own needs and self. On the last day of the schedule, put a reminder to schedule out the next six months. Make sure these dates are shared with relevant partners and helpers so that others can schedule around this time as well.

Feelings are meant to be transitory, yet they often end up "stuck" in us when we don't allow ourselves to express them. What are ways that you are comfortable showing your feelings around your family (e.g., crying while in control in front of your child)? What are ways that you might need to feel your feelings at a different time or place (e.g., postponing a challenging conversation until the morning)?

Reflect on what have you learned about your internal daily and monthly rhythms.
When do you have the most creative energy in your day and month?

_____

_____

_____

_____

_____

When do you tend to crash and when are the times you would most benefit from rest?

_____

_____

_____

_____

When are the best times to schedule events in which you socialize, talk, and move your energy outwards?

_____

_____

_____

_____

_____

Meeting your new self doesn't have to be a quiet and reflective task. It could instead consist of time to date yourself! Dating yourself is a chance to enjoy what you want to do without compromise: your favorite restaurant, your favorite appetizer, your favorite book to read while you eat. What are some self-dating ideas you can try?

I walk on my life path with intention, a brave heart, and steady footing.

Renée Trudeau, a women's self-love advocate and a mentor of mine, recommends planning to participate in a retreat every quarter. It could be a few hours of yoga and journaling, a meditation workshop, a weekend away at a retreat center, or even a spa day. It could also be two hours without the kiddo where you can sit, drink tea, color in an adult coloring book, and listen to a teaching. Write down some ideas, then challenge yourself to plan one retreat in the next three months to give yourself space to fill your cup.

_____

_____

_____

_____

_____

_____

_____

_____

_____

_____

_____

_____

_____

_____

_____

Imagine you are your own fan or coach on the sidelines of your life journey. What would you be saying to yourself at this moment? What sign would you want to see your fans holding up for you in the bleachers? Whom would you imagine standing there with you and cheering?

_____

_____

_____

_____

_____

_____

_____

_____

_____

_____

_____

_____

_____

_____

_____

_____

_____

_____

_____

_____

As you move forward creating community and relationships, you may also be challenged to confront systems of oppression—be it for the color of your skin, your gender, your sexuality, or otherwise. Experiencing microaggressions is incredibly taxing; consider how you might use rest or community to fortify yourself. If you are in a privileged position of observing some systems of oppression but not experiencing them, reflect on how you would like to use your privilege going forward. For ideas, check out the Resources section (page 168).

A Valuable Reminder

Remembering your personal values might
mean practicing moving away from societal
values of "busy" and "productive." Find a
way to represent your values in your house
or workspace to help you stay in touch with
them. You might make a pretty sign listing the
values, put them on a Post-It on your monitor
at work, or use a picture or a poem in a frame
to capture them. Take some time now to
create a representation of your values.

It's amazing how quickly we can end up taking on new jobs and tasks that fill up our schedule. Take a moment now to identify your "nonnegotiable" self-care activity—the one you do not want to drop no matter how busy you are. What will you need to do going forward to protect it?

Use all the space on this page to explore what comes to mind when you think about yourself. Use words, phrases, or sentences to capture whatever thoughts pop into your mind. When you are finished, reflect on what you've written. What do you notice about the tone? What do you notice about the themes? What do you see on your page that makes you feel good and proud?

Art Journaling

Take one of your kid's picture books they don't especially love. Turn it into an art journal! Gather up art supplies: watercolors, colored pencils, ink pens, glue, and magazines. Draw and write on a page of the book, adding your own doodles and drawings. If there are words in the book, consider covering certain words so that the ones that are left have particular meaning for you.

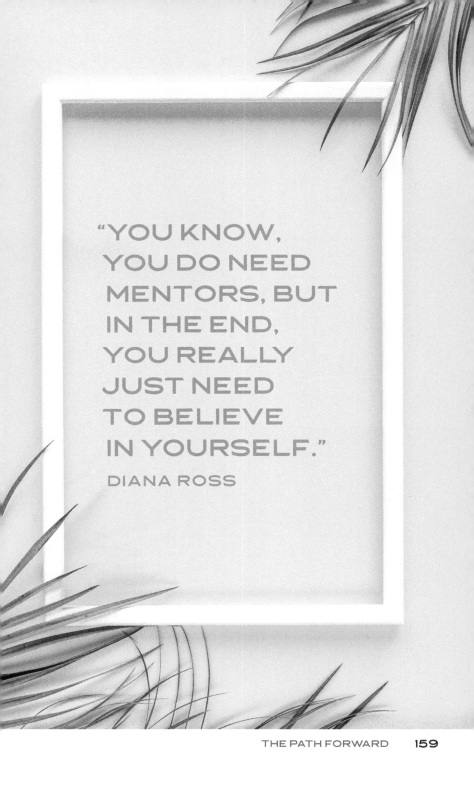

"YOU KNOW,
YOU DO NEED
MENTORS, BUT
IN THE END,
YOU REALLY
JUST NEED
TO BELIEVE
IN YOURSELF."

DIANA ROSS

Finding mentors who understand your life is an important way to get help in navigating the world. Sometimes mentors appear for us, and other times we have to intentionally seek them out. Whom do you already have in your life that serves as a mentor for you? Are there others you could reach out to? Jot down their names and describe what type of mentorship they could give you that would help.

We have different voices in our head: Our ego tends to function from fear and is constantly comparing us to others, while our wise mind uses both reason and emotion to find the truth around us. When you are quiet and listen to your wise mind, what do you hear it telling you?

Play Time (for You)

We have talked a lot about play and creativity as ways to get in touch with your inner voice and tap into joy. Assemble a creativity kit that you can have handy for those 20 minutes when the baby doesn't need attention. Gather art supplies, magazines, scissors, moldable clay, etc. Play with enjoying the process of creating using your kit and not just putting value on the final product.

Joy is considered a state as opposed to a fleeting emotion: a place you can inhabit and where you feel connected to something greater than yourself, appreciating your life and experiencing a calm and grounded happiness. Write down five things that you are grateful for. Remember: Gratitude does not mean ignoring hurts. Rather, practice tuning into gratitude while also offering yourself comfort for any sadness or pain.

We are at an end! You have read, reflected, tried new things, and inhabited your world in new ways. What tools have you discovered through our exploration that you most want to remember as you move forward? What would you want your future self to remember?

A FINAL WORD

Thank you for letting me be part of this period of discovery and reflection. You have deeply honored yourself in taking the time to explore new and old parts of yourself and how they show up in this period of mothering. You have spent time remembering what matters to you and integrating it into your new life. You've practiced connecting with the world around you more deeply and trying new ways of loving yourself. You have done hard work here, and I hope you can recognize that (without dismissing it, as we moms are wont to do!).

Each day, I wake up to the new mother that I am. New perspectives, new learning, deeper compassion, and richer self-love change who I am and how I show up in the world. I am not the woman with an infant, nor am I the woman with a toddler, but they are part of me, and the lessons and experiences I have lived shape how I live and love in my life today. My hope is that you allow yourself the time and energy to return to yourself again and again so you can live a life honoring your gifts, your importance, and your values, in this moment, right now.

Before I go, humor me one more time: Sit tall in your seat. Soften your belly. Place your hands overlapping over your heart. Now imagine the love of all the world's mothers is available and accessible to you. Imagine that love flowing into your hands and into your heart as a color—whatever color you wish. As you imagine this color of love and let it flow into you and fill you, remember that this boundless love is everywhere around you, and it's available to you in any moment. All you have to do to access it is remember that you are worthy of it.

RESOURCES

Mental Health and Well-being

General Information on Postpartum Mood Disorders

If you are having feelings that are making it hard to function—such as having difficulty sleeping, eating, leaving the house, or connecting with friends—please reach out for help. It isn't just postpartum depression that can happen after having a baby. We call them postpartum mood disorders (PPMDs): depression, anxiety, obsessive-compulsive disorder, and psychosis (e.g., hearing or seeing things others can't, experiencing feelings of paranoia, or having difficulty staying in touch with reality). They can all start any time in the first two years after having a baby. For more information on these conditions, check out Postpartum.net/learn-more.

Depression Questionnaire

The Edinberg Postnatal Depression Scale is a questionnaire you can take to gauge if you are experiencing symptoms of depression. It cannot diagnose you, but it might help you figure out if you need to reach out for help. Having a low score does not mean you are not depressed, so please don't let this discourage you from getting help. (You might be underreporting how bad your symptoms are because, as moms, we are pretty tough and can downplay our struggles.) You can take the questionnaire at Med.Stanford.edu/content/dam/sm/ppc/documents/DBP/EDPS_text_added.pdf

Postpartum Support

If you need speak to someone about what you are experiencing, you can visit Postpartum Support International at Postpartum.net or call them at 1-800-944-4773.

Finding a Therapist

Treating Postpartum Mood Disorders (PPMDs) requires special training. Make sure your therapist or psychiatrist has experience working with mothers suffering from PPMDs. Ask your provider what their training is, or use the directory from Postpartum Support International at Postpartum.net/get-help/providerdirectory.

Understanding and Relieving Stress

Here are several books and videos that can help with stress.

→ *The Pocket Guide to the Polyvagal Theory: The Transformative Power of Feeling Safe* by Stephen W. Porges

→ *Befriending Your Nervous System: Looking Through the Lens of Polyvagal Theory* by Deb Dana, LCSW

→ *The Body Keeps the Score: Brain, Mind, and Body in the Healing of Trauma* by Bessel van der Kolk, MD

Books for Well-being

→ *Sabbath: Finding Rest, Renewal, and Delight in Our Busy Lives* by Wayne Muller

→ *Radical Acceptance: Embracing Your Life with the Heart of a Buddha* by Tara Brach, PhD

→ *Yoga Journal Presents Restorative Yoga for Life: A Relaxing Way to De-Stress, Re-Energize and Find Balance* by Gail Boorstein Grossman, E-RYT 500, CYKT

Books on Racial Justice

→ *Me and White Supremacy* by Layla F. Saad

→ *White Tears/Brown Scars: How White Feminism Betrays Women of Color* by Ruby Hamad

→ *My Grandmother's Hands: Racialized Trauma and the Pathway to Mending Our Hearts and Bodies* by Resmaa Menakem

Mindfulness, Yoga, and Relaxation Practices

Yoga and Meditation Apps and Websites

→ Calm.com

→ Buddhify.com

→ Headspace.com

→ Yoga with Adrienne on YouTube.com

Breathing Exercise Examples

→ Square Breath: Exhale slowly and completely through your nose to begin. Let your belly relax out and down. Inhale slowly through your nose to a count of 4. Hold at the top of the breath for a count of 4. Slowly exhale through your mouth for a count of 4. Hold at the bottom of the breath for a count of 4. (You can try with a count of 2 or 6 instead of 4, depending on your lung capacity.)

→ Pursed Lip Breath: Purse your lips as though you are going to whistle; as an alternative, roll your tongue. Inhale through your nose for a count of 2. Exhale through your mouth (with lips pursed or tongue rolled) for a count of 4.

Mindful Eating Practice Example

1. Before you eat, notice your hunger sensation, how your mouth feels, and how your belly and stomach feel. Notice what emotions you are feeling (or wanting to avoid feeling, if that's the case).

2. Look at your food. Notice the texture and colors. Notice the aromas.

3. Take a small bite of food. Hold it in your mouth for just a moment before chewing. Notice your body's response

1. to the food in your mouth. Notice what it feels like on your tongue. Notice the flavor.

2. Chew once and stop. Notice the flavor. Notice your body's reaction. Notice the aromas. Notice the texture.

3. Continue chewing. Do not swallow immediately, but intentionally swallow (not out of habit) when you are ready.

4. Continue your meal at a slow and easy pace, giving attention to each bite.

5. At the end of your meal, notice again your hunger sensation and how your body feels.

Online Yoga Practices
→ Bed Yoga: YogaJournal.com/ practice/5-yoga-poses-morning-person/
→ Yoga Nidra meditations: InsightTimer. com/thestillpoint/guided-meditations/ yoga-nidra-for-sleep-and-rest and Youtu.be/-PxNLFJ91Io

Chanting Practices
You can turn any line or phrase into a chant to sing. Experiment with creating your own. "I am full of light," "I am safe and calm," "I am loved and am love," and, "Mother Earth holds me," are all examples you can try out.
You can also find information and practices for chanting online:
→ Chanting: HuffPost.com/entry/ chakra-chanting_b_1606147
→ Kundalini opening chant: SikhDharma.org/ the-adi-mantra

Understanding Your Body

I've talked a lot about the body-brain connection; here are some places you can delve into this topic in more detail.

Menstrual Cycle
→ Clue: HelloClue.com/articles/cycle-a-z/the-menstrual -cycle-more-than-just-the-period
→ Hormonology: MyHormonology.com/learn/ free-hormonology-ebooks/
→ Christiane Northrup M.D.: DrNorthrup.com/ wisdom-of-menstrual-cycle
→ *Code Red: Know Your Flow, Unlock Your Super- powers, and Create a Bloody Amazing Life. Period.* by Lisa Lister

Pelvic Floor
→ Pelvic Rehab: PelvicRehab.com
→ Jessie Mundell: JessieMundell.com

Your Relationship with Pleasure
→ *Becoming Cliterate: Why Orgasm Equality Matters— And How to Get It* by Dr. Laurie Mintz
→ *Come as You Are: The Surprising New Science that Will Transform Your Sex Life* by Emily Nagoski, PhD
→ *Shameless: A Case for Not Feeling Bad About Feeling Good (About Sex)* by Nadia Bolz-Weber
→ *For Goodness Sex: Changing the Way We Talk to Teens About Sexuality, Values, and Health* by Al Vernacchio
→ Sex Ed 101 Webinar with Erica Smith, sex educator: www.EricaSmithEAC.com

REFERENCES

Clear, James. "Core Values List." Accessed January 17, 2021. https://jamesclear.com/core-values.

Grasso, Hannah. "Archetypal Moon Energy; a Lunar Love Ritual." Gaia. June 4, 2018. Accessed January 2, 2021. https://www.gaia.com/article/four-archetypal-moon-energy-a-lunar-love-ritual.

Jay, Shani. "The Four Female Archetypes & How to Work With Them." She Rose Revolution. Accessed January 16, 2021. https://sheroserevolution.com/shanijay/the-four-female-archetypes/.

Jones, Kenneth and Tema Okun. "The Characteristics of White Supremacy Culture." Showing Up For Racial Justice. 2001. Accessed February 15, 2021. https://www.showingupforracialjustice.org/white-supremacy-culture-characteristics.html.

Lady Bird Physical Therapy. "The Pelvic Press." Accessed January 6, 2021. https://www.ladybirdpt.com/blog.
Pelvic Floor First. "Signs of a Pelvic Floor Problem." Accessed January 6, 2021. http://www.pelvicfloorfirst.org.au/pages/how-can-i-tellif-i-have-a-pelvic-floor-problem.html.

Slade, Margot. "Stephen W. Porges, PhD: Q&A About Freezing, fainting, and the 'Safe' Sounds of Music Therapy." Everyday Health. October 15, 2018. Accessed January 16, 2021. https://www.everydayhealth.com/wellness/united-states-of-stress/advisory-board/stephen-w-porges-phd-q-a/.
van Mersbergen, Miriam. "Viva La Vagus!" Choral Journal 55, 3 (October 2014). Accessed January 17, 2021. https://www.memphis.edu/vecl/pdfs/viva_la_vagus.pdf.

Acknowledgments

Thank you to Wesley Chiu and the team at Rockridge Press for working with me to make this resource available to new moms. Thanks to my editor, Adrian Potts, for his wonderful insight and guidance.

I am so grateful to the mentors my career journey introduced me to who led me here: Dr. Kathy Garnet, Dr. Deborah Tharinger, Dr. Krista Jordan, Kelly Inselmann, Renée Trudeau, and Jeanne Bunker.

To the matriarchs in my own family—my mother, my aunt, and my grandmother—for their love. Shannon, Lindsay, Stefanie and Christine—love you. (Dad, you always said I'd publish a book!) To my women friends: You make me feel loved, seen, and grounded.

Paul: You're the only person I'd ever want to quarantine with and still want more of. Kate and Jacob: You guys are hilarious, loving, and my favorite people.

Thank you all for birthing this version of me.

About the Author

Sarah Griesemer, PhD, is a licensed psychologist and certified therapist in treating postpartum mood disorders. In her private practice, she specializes in providing therapy to women, especially those who are feelers, therapists, healers, and new moms. She is dedicated to teaching and runs training groups, supervises students, and has taught and lectured at the University of Texas at Austin, among other places. She and her partner have two kids and a small menagerie of animals in their home in Austin, TX. You can find her empowering messages for moms on Instagram @hellomamathy or at her website www.Mamathy.com.